WORDS *of* HOPE and HEALING

GRIEF *after* HOMICIDE
Surviving, Mourning, Reconciling

Alan D. Wolfelt, Ph.D.

Companion
PRESS

An imprint of the Center for Loss and Life Transition | Fort Collins, Colorado

Companion Press is an imprint of the Center for Loss and Life Transition, 3735 Broken Bow Road, Fort Collins, Colorado 80526.

26   25   24   23   22   21   6   5   4   3   2   1

ISBN: 978-1-61722-303-7

CONTENTS

WELCOME

"There are no great people in this world, only great challenges which ordinary people rise to meet."
— William F. Halsey, Jr.

Someone you care about has died by homicide. I'm deeply sorry for your terrible loss.

As you know, homicide creates a grief like no other. Your normal and necessary grief has been made naturally complicated by the horrible circumstances of the death. What those circumstances are will vary widely among the readers who find their way to this book. Homicide is the act of one human killing another, whether intentionally (murder), unintentionally (manslaughter), or sometimes ambiguously, in the case of uncertain or suspicious causes of death, as well as some military deaths. No matter where the death of your loved one falls on this spectrum, I welcome you to this important discussion and source of support.

My first goal in writing this book is to help you feel seen, safe, and comforted. Our culture isn't very good at acknowledging and supporting grief in general, and it's especially bad at helping people affected by stigmatized types of death. Unfairly, deaths by homicide carry the burden of such a stigma. Even when the people who died in these awful situations are entirely innocent in what happened, and even though the friends and family members left behind are not to blame, survivors often experience social discomfort (and are sometimes even ostracized) because of the circumstances of the death.

Have you had friends and family members avoid you since the death? Have you felt judged in any way about what happened, or have others made you feel ashamed? If so, you have been victimized and isolated by harmful cultural norms. But I see you, and I'm here to talk to you about this death and your grief openly, honestly, and compassionately.

My second goal is to help you navigate your complicated grief and mourn actively. While no one can undo the death or take away your pain, there are ways of approaching and expressing your grief that will help you not only cope but go on to find hope and healing. I've been a grief counselor for more than forty years, and I've had the honor of being entrusted to companion many hurting souls in the aftermath of homicide. These survivors have been my teachers. And they've asked me to share with you their hard-earned wisdom about surviving your grief in the early weeks and months, befriending it when you're ready, and in the longer term, integrating it into your ongoing life so that you can continue to live well, with meaning and purpose.

While some of your friends and family members may not be supporting you right now, you are not alone. It might help you to know that a surprising number of people in your community may have survived a similar loss. In North America, many hundreds of thousands of people die each year from accidents (including motor-vehicle crashes), drug overdoses, gun-related violence, and other forms of sudden, premature, and often violent death. Of course, not all of these deaths are homicides, but a significant portion are. And among those that don't meet the legal criteria for homicide prosecution are many deaths that friends and family members consider unjust, unnecessary, and caused in some way, at least in part, by the actions (or inactions) of another person.

So it bears repeating: You are not alone. Your fellow homicide grievers can help you. This book can help you. With a little education, your friends and family members can help you. You can help yourself. And there are other sources of support we'll talk about soon.

There is help, and there is hope. Let's get started.

IN THE IMMEDIATE AFTERMATH

*"Being safe is about being seen and heard and allowed
to be who you are and to speak your truth."*

— Rachel Naomi Remen

If you're reading this book shortly after the death of a loved one by homicide, I want you to consider yourself in emotional and spiritual intensive care.

You have sustained a life-threatening emotional injury— something catastrophic, excruciatingly painful, and assaulting to the very core of your being. If you suffered a similarly grave physical injury, you would be rushed to the hospital and tended to with a great deal of attention and concern. That's the level of emotional and spiritual care you need and deserve right now.

Allow others to take care of you. Ask for help. Give yourself as much rest and recuperation as possible. Take time off work. Let housework slide. In the early weeks and months after the death, don't expect—indeed, don't try—to carry on with your normal routine.

For homicide survivors, feelings of anxiety and unsafety can be especially pronounced in the early days. Our bodies are programmed to feel tense and afraid in dangerous situations. This natural "fight-or-flight" response helps protect us from harm. Your body may be interpreting what happened to the person you love as a threat to you. And your mind may be returning over and over again to images or thoughts of violence or peril associated with the circumstances of the death. While normal, these thoughts make you feel anxious and unsafe. You may be having trouble getting through your day, sleeping, or going out in public.

You can't begin to cope with your grief, mourn, and heal until you feel safer. Safety has to come first. Consider what would make you feel safer right now. Do you need to stay at someone else's house for a while? Would it help you to see a counselor this week to defuse any overwhelming fears? Would you like some extra help watching over your children or taking care of necessary chores right now?

Again, ask for help, and do whatever you need to do to create a living situation and daily routine that makes you feel as safe and secure as possible today, tomorrow, and for the immediate future. These are your most essential immediate tasks.

TRAUMATIC GRIEF

*"Trauma is a fact of life. It does not, however,
have to be a life sentence."*
— Peter A. Levine

Before we discuss traumatic grief, let's define grief and mourning.

Grief is everything we think and feel on the inside after we experience a life loss. Commonly, grief from any kind of loss includes a mixture of feelings of shock, numbness, disorientation, anxiety, anger, sadness, guilt, and other emotions. When we're grieving, this mixture can change from hour to hour and day to day.

Grief also includes expressing our thoughts and feelings outside of ourselves. Crying is the hallmark expression of grief. Other grief behaviors include talking about what happened, hugging or holding others, writing in a grief journal, and sharing on social media. Collectively, all of these outward grief actions are called mourning. Mourning, in other words, is grief expressed.

Grief is normal and necessary. It's essentially our love for the person who died in a different form. Mourning is grief in motion, and it's also essential because it's how we move toward healing.

So what is traumatic grief? Traumatic grief is a type of grief caused by a traumatic event.

Even if you didn't witness what happened, you and the friends and family members of the person who died by homicide are suffering the aftermath of a traumatic event. The traumatic nature of the loss you experienced, and all of your thoughts and feelings about what happened—especially how it happened—naturally color every aspect of the grief that follows.

Basically, the traumatic event itself is part of your grief. But it is not the totality of your grief.

Homicide creates a two-part grief experience: one focused on the manner of the death itself, and one focused on the fact that someone you care about has died and will no longer be present to you in your ongoing life. Both of these parts of your traumatic grief need and deserve special attention and care.

No manner of sudden, premature death is easy to accept and grieve. Unexpected, premature, nonviolent deaths (such as the heart-attack death of a middle-aged person) are difficult.

Expected premature deaths (such as the death of a young person to cancer) are also heartbreaking. And even expected, timely, peaceful deaths (such as when a very elderly person dies in their sleep) naturally give rise to sorrow and grief. The more unexpected, premature, and violent the loss, however, the more likely you are to experience traumatic grief.

DO I HAVE PTSD?

You might be wondering if your traumatic grief is the same as PTSD. Post-traumatic stress disorder, or PTSD, is a term used to describe the psychological condition that survivors of a violent event sometimes experience. (I prefer to call it PTS, because it's not so much a disorder as it is a normal human response to an abnormally traumatic experience.)

Grievers with PTSD often have nightmares or scary, intrusive thoughts about the terrible experience their loved one went through. They may try to stay away from anything that reminds them of the frightening experience. They typically feel angry and may be unable to care about or trust other people. They are often constantly on the lookout for danger and get very upset when something happens without warning. Their anxiety level is continually heightened.

It's true that PTSD and traumatic grief have a lot in common. Yet many of you reading this book will have traumatic grief but not full-blown PTSD. You may have anxiety and anger. You may think about the circumstances of the death often. You may be in great pain. But if you are still able to function in your daily life and interact lovingly with others, you may not have PTSD. The chart on the following page may help you understand how similar the two can be. Still, you are traumatized and in need of special care and consideration, both from yourself and from others.

PTSD VERSUS TRAUMATIC GRIEF

SYMPTOM	PTSD	TRAUMATIC GRIEF
Thoughts or perception about the event/loss	✓	✓
Images of the event/loss	✓	✓
Dreams about the event/loss	✓	✓
Illusions or hallucinations	✓	✓
Dissociative flashbacks	✓	Sometimes
Psychological or physical reactions to cues	✓	✓
An inability to remember significant aspects of the event	✓	Sometimes
Avoiding thoughts, feelings, conversations, places, or people that are reminders	✓	✓
Persistent and negative beliefs about self, others, or the world	✓	Sometimes
Persistent, distorted thoughts about the cause or consequences of the event/loss	✓	Sometimes
Persistent negativity	✓	Sometimes
Markedly diminished interest or participation in significant activities	✓	✓
Feelings of detachment or estrangement from others; self-isolating behavior	✓	✓
Persistent inability to experience positive emotions; anhedonia	✓	✓
Difficulty sleeping	✓	✓
Irritability or anger outbursts; explosive emotions	✓	✓
Difficulty concentrating; disorganization, confusion	✓	✓
Hyper-vigilance	✓	Sometimes
Exaggerated startle response; anxiety, panic, fear	✓	✓

If you think you may be experiencing PTSD, please do make an appointment with your primary-care provider and/or a compassionate grief counselor. You may need therapy and/or medication for a time to help you feel safer and cope with your day-to-day life. What's more, you will need to get help for your PTSD before you can effectively engage with your grief and mourning. As I said earlier, a sense of safety has to come first.

Don't think you are "weak" if this traumatic event and its repercussions have overwhelmed your coping resources. Don't feel ashamed if you need to seek professional help. Often it is in acknowledging our helplessness that we ultimately become helpful to ourselves.

PART 1:

YOUR GRIEF OVER THE CIRCUMSTANCES OF THE HOMICIDE DEATH

"Here is the world. Beautiful and terrible things will happen."
— Frederick Buechner

The part of your grief focused on the traumatic event of the death itself may include a wide range and degree of thoughts and feelings. In fact, many homicide grievers have shared with me their worry that they were going crazy because their thoughts and moods felt so dramatic and unlike their baseline. If that's how you feel, don't worry, you're not going crazy—you're grieving a traumatic death.

The feelings in the list that follows are common in normal grief as well, but you're likely to find them stronger and more extreme in a traumatic loss situation:

PRONOUNCED, PROLONGED SHOCK AND PSYCHIC NUMBING
This is a normal and necessary phase in homicide grief because it is nature's way of protecting you from the full

force of a terrible reality all at once. These feelings are like bubble wrap. They cushion you, and they muffle the entirety of the truth for a while. If you're still experiencing shock and numbness, rest assured that if you work on safety and then active mourning, bit by bit and over time you'll embrace the reality of what happened as you're ready.

HELPLESSNESS AND POWERLESSNESS

Nothing makes us feel more helpless than being unable to prevent the suffering and death of the people we love. We want to protect them, but we can't. As you are probably aware, homicide grief heightens these normal feelings of lack of control. The more terrible the suffering and death, the more powerless you're likely to feel. Actively engaging with the six needs of mourning, which we'll review soon, will help you eventually surrender to that which is beyond your control, especially in matters of life and death.

FEAR, ANXIETY, DISSOCIATION

The first part of your two-part grief is largely about fear. What happened to the person you love was no doubt scary, and it's normal for you to think about it, wonder about it, and imagine it. The means of death probably made you feel unsafe or anxious in the early days after the death, and those effects can linger for a long time. Your body's normal fight-or-flight system can get stuck in anxiety and worry.

Expressing and processing your fears aloud as they arise helps to soften them.

Dissociation is a psychological term that means a sense of disconnection from your thoughts, feelings, memories, surroundings, or even yourself. It's common after traumatic events. If you feel separate from your life, if what's happening seems surreal, or if you feel like you're going through the motions but you're not really "there," you are probably experiencing normal, temporary dissociation as a result of the circumstances of the death. If these feelings are especially troubling to you, however, or are interfering with your ability to function day-to-day or strongly persisting for months, it's a good idea to see a counselor who can support you as you work on reintegration.

EXPLOSIVE EMOTIONS

The explosive emotions of anger, hate, blame, terror, resentment, and rage may be volatile yet natural parts of your grief over the manner of the death. It's normal to be angry when someone you care about is harmed by someone else, let alone killed. We instinctively believe in every person's basic human right to live their life without someone taking it from them. When this right is violated, it's normal to feel explosive emotions. When you're feeling angry, it might help you to recognize that your explosive emotions are essentially a form of survival-oriented protest. When we don't like something that's happened, it's natural to get mad about it. That's because we're protesting a reality we don't want. Our impulse is to reject the unwanted truth. It feels better to be mad than sad because explosive emotions feel more active and powerful. But over time, befriending any explosive emotions you may have been experiencing will help you understand that they are often masking necessary sorrow.

PHYSICAL SYMPTOMS

Among the most common physical responses to loss are trouble with sleeping and low energy. You may be finding it hard to get to sleep, or you may be waking up in the middle of the night and finding it hard to fall back asleep. During the daytime, you might feel deeply lethargic. Our bodies feel grief, too, and since your grief is traumatic, your body may actually feel traumatized, as if you've been hit by a wrecking ball. You may experience muscle aches and pains, shortness of breath, tightness in the throat and chest, digestive problems, heart palpitations, nausea, headaches, and more.

If you're having physical issues of any kind, it's a good idea to see your primary-care provider. They can ensure you don't have a serious underlying condition, and they may be able to help with your sleep issues and bodily pain. They might also talk to you about anti-anxiety medication, antidepressants,

Grief after Homicide

and/or therapy—all of which could be strong pillars of your short-term care plan.

SEEKING INFORMATION AND UNDERSTANDING

When it comes to the death of someone loved, our minds naturally want to know what happened, and why. It's part of our need to come to terms with the reality. First we have to understand it with our heads, and over time we come to understand it more deeply, with our hearts.

After a homicide death, the need for information and clarity can feel particularly strong.

You may want to know the details of what happened and when. If that's how you feel, it's perfectly reasonable to pursue learning more information. Within reason, the more you know about what happened, the more readily you will be able to acknowledge and accept what happened. It may help you to be appropriately assertive in seeking information and asking for ongoing updates from investigators.

If you want to, obtain a copy of the crime report and/or autopsy. (If you do, I strongly encourage you to read this information in the company of an empathetic friend or trusted counselor.) Contact the investigating agency and ask who's in charge of the case. Ask if charges are being considered and why. Ask if there's a victims' advocacy program to help you with emotional, legal, and financial challenges your family may be experiencing. Ask to be informed as the case moves through hearings, arraignment, trial, and sentencing. If you're not feeling up to all this, ask a friend of the family to be your liaison with the criminal justice system and to bring you pertinent news.

Conversely, you might find yourself wanting to avoid all details about the event of the death. If this is how you feel, it's also OK. You don't need to know everything about how the death happened in order to accept the fact of the death, but you will need to find other ways to acknowledge and embrace the reality and to make sure you're not fundamentally trying to deny the truth about what happened or go around your necessary grief.

INTERACTING WITH LAW ENFORCEMENT, THE JUDICIAL SYSTEM, AND THE MEDIA

Beyond accessing the criminal-justice system to seek information and understanding, depending on the circumstances of the death you may find yourself unavoidably intertwined with criminal proceedings and media coverage— sometimes for a period of months or even years. If you're in this situation, your two-part grief is likely to split into three-part grief, with the third part unavoidably focused on the public spectacle and process. This third part is difficult and draining, and will require special care all its own. I urge you to seek extra support and set up systems to manage all of it.

Grief after Homicide

If the death resulted in prominent or ongoing media coverage, you and your family may need media-related care. Over and over you may hear about the death on TV, social media, or online news sites. This phenomenon tends to make families feel a strange sense of dislocation, as if the death that intimately impacted their lives also happened on another, more abstract plane. (This can be part of the dissociation experience we talked about on page 15.) Some families find that in being open with the media, they are able to share their personal stories in ways that help both them and the community mourn. Others find that to mourn and heal, they must withdraw and mourn more privately, among close family and friends. When necessary, be assertive with media representatives. Tell them what your limits are in terms of talking about the death. Ask not to be contacted or to be contacted through an attorney or specially designated advocate. If you clearly spell out your preferred boundaries, most media representatives will respect them. If they don't, you might need to consult legal authorities regarding your rights.

Above all, remember that even if the public realm has laid claim to this death, it is still first and foremost your personal loss. Focus on your family's grief. Focus on your own physical, cognitive, emotional, social, and spiritual wellbeing. Do what feels best and healing for you It's important for you to do what is right for you and your family.

HOMICIDE GRIEF AND SECONDARY VICTIMIZATION

Your family is a victim of homicide. Unfortunately, as you grieve you will probably be further wounded by what is called "secondary victimization." This is what happens when you encounter situations in which your loss is handled insensitively by the media, law enforcement, or others. You may be blamed or shamed, or your feelings may be ill-considered or overridden. Even when others are trying to help you, their inconsiderate approach may cause further trauma. You've already been torn apart, and now salt is being poured on your wounds.

If and when you experience moments of secondary victimization, I urge you to express your emotions. It's healthy to be open and honest about how these situations make you feel, both as they are happening and later, as you are debriefing with a trusted friend or family member. Actively mourn these moments as soon as you can after they happen (in addition to while they are happening, when possible). Be sure to talk through these experiences whenever your feelings about them arise, even long after they've occurred. The more you outwardly process secondary victimization experiences, the more fully these exacerbated wounds will heal—and the more grace you will be able to extend to the often-unwitting perpetrators of these experiences.

HOMICIDE GRIEF AND GRIEF OVERLOAD

Grief overload is what you feel when you experience too many significant losses all at once or in a relatively short period of time. Sometimes, unimaginably, more than one loved one is killed in the same incident. Over the years I've had the unfortunate opportunity to companion several families in this terrible situation. And sometimes multiple losses occur in quick succession. Our minds and hearts have enough trouble coping with one loss at a time, but when they have to deal with multiple losses simultaneously, the grief often seems especially chaotic and defeating.

The homicide death you are grieving puts you at risk of grief overload because it is an immense grief to begin with. If other losses in your life end up overlapping with the homicide death, you may understandably feel like you're struggling to survive.

If you find yourself in this unfortunate situation, a professional grief counselor could help you create a plan for coping in the short-term and giving each loss its own necessary mourning attention in the longer term. It may take months and possibly years of active, engaged, committed mourning for you to feel that all of your losses are being reconciled and you are achieving momentum toward a future of meaning and purpose. Starting sessions with a therapist now may provide you with the support and structure you need immediately as well as help you start off on the best long-term path.

PART 2:

YOUR ONGOING GRIEF

*"The reality is you will grieve forever. You will not 'get over'
the loss of a loved one; you will learn to live with it. You will heal
and you will rebuild yourself around the loss you have suffered. You
will be whole again, but you will never be the same again.
Nor should you be the same nor should you want to."*
— Elisabeth Kübler-Ross

Again, grief is everything we think and feel on the inside
after we experience a life loss. Because of the two-part nature
of the grief caused by homicide, your grief is a mixture of
thoughts and feelings about the traumatic circumstances of
the death (part 1) as well as your thoughts and feelings about
the forever, ongoing absence of the person who died (part 2).

So, your ongoing grief is the second part of your two-part
grief. It's the part of your grief you would experience no matter
how the person you love had died at this point in your life.

Of course, in real life grief doesn't actually split into two
parts so neatly. It's all intertwined. On any given day, you

may not be able to tell which of your thoughts and feelings fit into which of these buckets. Rest assured, teasing them apart like this is not necessary. As long as you understand the basic concept of two-part grief, that's enough for you to embrace and attend to your special needs as a homicide griever.

The list below contains a number of influences, thoughts, and feelings that are likely to shape your ongoing grief.

YOUR UNIQUE LIFE

You've probably realized already that your ongoing grief is shaped by many variables other than the cause of the death. Your unique personality, the personality of the person who died, the closeness and qualities of your relationship with the person who died, your religious or spiritual background, your physical health, your past experiences with loss, how much support you have around you, and other factors will also play a big part in determining what your grief journey will be like. Depending on where you are in your grief journey, right now it may seem like the cause of the death overshadows most or all of these other influences. That's normal. Over time, your grief will naturally become less about the manner of the death and more about the matter of the death and the continuing love you have for the person you lost.

SEARCHING AND YEARNING

When someone you love dies, it's normal to search and yearn for them. For a period of months (or even much longer), your mind may continue to look for the person—in your home, in crowds, in places that they used to frequent. You may expect them to phone you or to walk through the door at any moment. This happens because it simply takes time for our minds and hearts to fully process and accept the reality and finality of the death.

Yearning, too, is normal. This is the feeling of missing the person. They're gone, and you want them back. You will never completely stop wishing your special person could be here with you again, but over time this feeling will naturally become less powerful and instead give way to acceptance that they are gone, though the love remains.

UNFINISHED BUSINESS

Sudden deaths of any kind often create ongoing feelings of unfinished business. Were there things you wanted to say to the person who died, but you never got the chance? Were there mistakes you made that you'd hoped to rectify but now can't? Were there tasks or plans uncompleted or wishes unfulfilled? If so, you probably feel the frustration and sorrow of unfinished business. Over time, actively expressing these feelings will help you integrate them into your ongoing life.

GUILT AND REGRET

These feelings are parts of normal ongoing grief for many (but not all) people and are often more pronounced following an unexpected death. You may feel "if-onlys" related to the circumstances of the death (If only he hadn't gone there on that day…) and/or related to common life circumstances (If only I'd said I love you the last time we spoke, If only we'd followed through on that plan, etc.).

In addition, you may experience survivor guilt, which stems from wondering why the other person died instead of you/ someone else or wishing it was you instead. It's natural to feel this way, especially if you felt responsible for the person who died, and expressing these thoughts and feelings is part of how you will begin to reconcile your grief.

SADNESS AND DESPAIR

Sadness may be the most hurtful feeling on your journey through grief. Nobody wants to be sad. Sadness drains all pleasure from our lives. Sadness makes us feel bad. But sadness is also a natural, authentic emotion after the death of someone loved. Someone precious in your life is now gone. Of course you are sad. Of course you feel deep sorrow. Allowing yourself to not only feel sad but befriend your sadness is, in large part, what your journey toward healing is all about.

Because of the circumstances of the homicide death, your sadness will understandably emanate from the "how" of

Grief after Homicide

the death as well as the ongoing absence of the person who died. Like many aspects of your grief, your sadness will have two parts. Again, it's impossible and unnecessary to try to totally separate the two, but mourning your sadness over both aspects of the loss will help you integrate your grief and move toward healing.

THREE FORGOTTEN TRUTHS

In our culture today, there are three forgotten truths about grief. Learning about them has helped many traumatized grievers I've companioned over the years.

1. **You must say hello before you can say goodbye.**
   Saying goodbye to the physical presence of the person you loved is a journey. You will find that before you can fully understand and accept this goodbye, you must first say hello to the reality and circumstances of the death.

2. **You must make friends with the darkness before you can enter the light.**
   In grief, making friends with the darkness means accepting and spending time with your dark emotions and allowing yourself to feel your natural pain in doses.

3. **You must go backward before you can go forward.**
   Grief by its very nature is a recursive process. This means It spirals back on itself. It is repetitive. You will probably need to

go backward to reexamine the circumstances of the death and possibly other issues—such as your relationship with the person who died, feelings of unfinished businesses, and any regrets or guilt—many times. It's normal and necessary, especially in traumatic grief, to go backward over and over again before you begin to feel any momentum carrying you forward.

MOURNING YOUR GRIEF

"There is sacredness in tears. They are not the mark of weakness, but of power. They speak more eloquently than ten thousand tongues. They are the messengers of overwhelming grief, of deep contrition, and of unspeakable love."

— Washington Irving

Mourning is the act of expressing your grief. As we've said, it's grief in motion, and it's essential to healing.

Another way to think of mourning is that it's the "work" of grief. It's what you actively *do* with your grief. It's how you share it outside of yourself. It's how you give it a voice and momentum.

While the circumstances of your loss and grief are unique, it's also true that all people in grief share a set of six mourning needs. Engaging with them is how you will do the work of your grief. Unlike the stages of grief you may have heard about (a concept I don't believe is that accurate or helpful), the six needs of mourning are more active "to-dos" than passive, prescriptive feelings.

The six needs of mourning are not orderly or predictable. You will probably jump around in random fashion while working on them. You will address each need when you are ready to do so. And often you will be working on more than one need at a time.

YOUR SIX NEEDS OF MOURNING

Need 1: Acknowledge the circumstances and reality of the death

Need 2: Embrace the pain of the death and the loss

Need 3: Tell your story of the death and the life of the person who died

Need 4: Develop a new self-identity

Need 5: Search for meaning

Need 6: Receive and accept help from others

Mourning homicide grief is definitely not easy. But know this: If you are able to muster the courage to intentionally and actively work on the six needs of mourning, you will heal. And you will eventually love and live fully again. Remember, you are not alone, and there are no rewards for speed. Millions of others have not only survived the homicide death of a loved one, they've chosen to truly live.

You can, too.

Now let's talk about each of the six needs of mourning and how you can use them to engage your two-part grief.

MOURNING NEED 1. ACKNOWLEDGE THE CIRCUMSTANCES AND REALITY OF THE DEATH

You are tasked with coming to terms with the reality of both the manner of your loved one's death and the fact that they are no longer alive. Both are terrible realities to encounter and eventually accept. But still, that is what you must do—in small doses, slowly and over time—while being supported with tender loving care.

In the early days after the death, you may have actively worked on this mourning need by learning the details of what happened, spending time with the body, sharing the news with others, and participating in a meaningful funeral ceremony. Over the long run, you actively acknowledge the death by talking to others about it, being open and honest about what happened (including using terms that feel accurate to you, such as "killed" or "died by homicide"), using the name of the person who died, visiting the final resting place, and other actions that continue to help you confront and accept the reality.

If you find yourself replaying the circumstances of the death over and over in your mind, know that this replay is your brain's way of trying to grasp what happened. Such replay can be normal and necessary in helping you acknowledge this death. But if these thoughts are overly harrowing or intrusive, you may need professional help in dealing with them. Sometimes the circumstances of homicide deaths are just too traumatizing for mourners to integrate without the support of a skilled trauma counselor.

While the need to acknowledge the circumstances of a homicide death comes at an earlier phase of Mourning Need 1, fully acknowledging the realities of life without the person who died takes much longer. Yet, over time, you will come to find that your grief is as much or more about the life of the person who died than it is about the terrible circumstances of their death.

MOURNING NEED 2: EMBRACE THE PAIN OF THE DEATH AND THE LOSS

For survivors, as you probably know all too well, homicide deaths cause unimaginable pain. Yet you will need to slowly—ever so slowly—dose yourself in embracing that pain. If you were to allow in all the pain at once, you could not survive.

People with painful chronic medical conditions are taught not to tighten around the pain but to relax and allow the pain to be present. When pain is resisted, it intensifies. You don't want to fight with your pain—you want to allow it into your soul bit by bit so that eventually you can move from darkness into light.

What does embracing pain mean? It means allowing yourself to be with it and feel it and understanding the appropriateness of the fact that you're in pain. When it tries to get your attention, stop what you are doing—or make an appointment with the pain for later in the day—and let it wash over and through you. When this is happening, you can also actively mourn the pain by expressing it outside of yourself. Sob if you feel like sobbing. Call a friend to talk about what you're feeling. Write in a grief journal. Unburden yourself to a grief counselor.

Even though your pain over both the cause of the death and your ongoing loss is no doubt deep and vast, you do have the strength to befriend it. I know this because your pain is a normal and natural part of your love for the person who died. And as you begin to give kind, compassionate attention to your pain, you will simultaneously begin to realize that it's actually not so scary and overwhelming. It's your love in a different form. You will come to understand that it's necessary and even good to say hello to the pain, get acquainted with it, and accommodate it into your ongoing life.

I encourage you to embrace and express your pain a little bit today. I encourage you to embrace and express your pain a little bit tomorrow. As you repeat this process over and over again, the pain will start to soften, and the love and gratitude you feel for the life of the person who died will slowly expand to fill its place.

DOSING YOUR MOURNING

In traumatic loss situations such as homicide, it's absolutely essential to remember that you can only embrace and express your grief in small doses, bit by bit, over time. Your mourning commitment is to encounter your grief each day as it arises, give it some awareness and time, and then turn your attention to other things.

In other words, you must encounter your grief then evade your grief. You work, then you take the time you need to rest and restore. It is only through this back-and-forth movement that you can eventually come to reconcile yourself to your terrible loss. If you don't give yourself ample self-care and recuperation in between doses of active mourning, you will likely burn out and may well sink into clinical depression.

And if you ever feel stuck in active mourning—like you can't disengage from your deep grief for parts of each day or you just can't get away from your grief enough to carry out the necessary tasks of daily life—that's a sign that you need extra help. I recommend making an appointment with a grief counselor right away. Remember, there is help, and there is hope.

MOURNING NEED 3: TELL YOUR STORY OF THE DEATH AND THE LIFE OF THE PERSON WHO DIED

Mourning Need 3 is about remembering. It's about spending time immersing yourself in stories about and memories of the life of the person who died. It's also about the story of the death, which in this case was likely a traumatic event— an event that you were not present for but that is traumatic to your psyche nonetheless. (If you were present for the death itself or the immediate aftermath, it's important that you process what you experienced with the help of a skilled trauma counselor.)

While Mourning Need 1 is about acknowledging the facts of the death, Mourning Need 3 involves coming to an understanding about what happened and creating a narrative that you can live with. As we've said, it's normal to think about the death itself, imagine what happened, ask questions, and possibly gather information. All of those tasks help meet Mourning Need 1. But once you've decided you have all the information you need (or are likely to get), you will begin to arrive at a more rehearsed, stable understanding of what happened. At this point you may decide what you *choose* to believe about any unknowable moments or nuances of the death. In other words, to some degree, you get to create your story of what happened.

This is the story of the death that you'll carry forward with you into your ongoing life. When you're ready, this is the story you'll be able to tell to others and perhaps pass along to future generations. I'm not advocating for denying what actually happened, because acknowledging any known realities is your first critical mourning need. Rather, I'm suggesting that you can choose to fill in gaps, embellish, and stitch the known parts together in ways that comfort you and ultimately give you a degree of peace. For example, maybe you decide the death was painless. Maybe you choose to believe that a guardian angel was present. Or maybe you imagine the person who died wrapped in your abiding love. Whatever details, nuances, or synchronicities you weave into your story of the death, know that that is your right.

Of course, because of your two-part grief, the work of Mourning Need 3 is not only about the death but also about the life. When someone loved dies, they live on in us through memory. Whenever you spend time looking at photos or watching videos from the person's life, you're working on this need. Ditto when you go through memorabilia, make a memory box (a special box containing photos, souvenirs, etc.), and pass along keepsakes to others grieving the person's death. Getting together with close friends and family to share memories and tell stories about the life of the person who died is another important way.

To move toward healing, you need to actively remember the person who died and commemorate the life they lived. Never let anyone take your memories away in a misguided attempt to save you from pain. Help them understand that spending time with memories, photos, and objects that link you to the person who died is good. Remembering the past makes hoping for the future possible.

USING CEREMONY AND RITUAL TO ENGAGE WITH THE SIX NEEDS OF MOURNING

The funeral or memorial ceremony for the person who died may have already taken place, but you can still continue to use ceremony to help yourself cope with your grief and move toward healing. I often say, "When everyday words and actions are inadequate, turn to ceremony."

For example, you could hold a small candle-lighting ceremony in your home on the birthday of the person who died. Or you could have a tree-planting ceremony in your yard to mark the anniversary of the death. Or you can carry out small, private daily rituals all on your own, such as reading a certain prayer when you wake up each morning or making an entry in a gratitude journal when you climb into bed each night.

Rituals are effective mourning actions because they often engage many, if not all, of the needs of mourning at the same time. What's more, they often include a "secret sauce" made up of intentionality, symbolism, and spirituality,

I encourage you to add rituals big and small, formal and informal, to your work of mourning. They will enhance your healing.

MOURNING NEED 4: DEVELOP A NEW SELF-IDENTITY

Part of your self-identity was formed by the relationship you had with the person who died. You may have gone from being a "wife" to a "widow" or from a "parent" to a "bereaved parent." The way you defined yourself and the way others define you may have changed.

What's more, your self-identity may now include associations with the homicide death. While you wish this weren't so and you should not accept completely defining yourself in relation to the manner of the death, what happened is now a significant part of your life story. Coming to terms with this fact and integrating it into who you want to be is part of the work of this mourning need.

Essentially, now you need to re-anchor yourself, to reconstruct your self-identity. This is arduous and painful work. One of your biggest challenges may be to recreate yourself in the face of the loss of who you once were. Let me assure you that you can do this.

Grief after Homicide

Who were you? Who are you? Who do you want to be moving forward? How can you use this reset—unwanted, yes, but a reset nonetheless—to make new or adjusted life choices that are closely and intentionally aligned with what really matters to you?

Talking about your self-identity quest with others, spending time thinking and planning, journaling about your interests and desires, dipping your toe into new activities you've long been interested in or renewing old passions, and rescheduling your days to better care for yourself and your soul are all ways to actively engage with this mourning need.

Many mourners find that as they work on Mourning Need 4, they ultimately discover some positive changes in themselves, such as becoming more caring or less judgmental. The homicide death that so unwantedly barged into your life story can, in some ways, help you grow and even improve some aspects of your life. I understand that this is growth you would gladly give back in exchange for just one more minute with the person who died, but here you are, and it is growth you have the bittersweet chance to enjoy nonetheless.

MOURNING NEED 5. SEARCH FOR MEANING

The search for meaning is a long and painful process, especially after a homicide death. How can you possibly find meaning in such a tragedy? Yet nonetheless, when someone loved dies suddenly and violently, it's normal to question the meaning and purpose of what happened as well as the meaning and purpose of life in general.

"Why?" questions may surface uncontrollably and often precede "How?" questions. "Why did this happen?" comes before "How will I go on living?" Some people may tell you that asking "Why?" doesn't do you any good. These people are usually unfamiliar with the experience of traumatic grief. Try to reach out to people who can create a supportive atmosphere for your natural search for meaning.

Many people touched by homicide loss come to realize that there is no meaning to the tragedy itself. No rhyme or reason. No justice. Death at the hands of another person is wrong and senseless, period. But these grievers also learn, over time, that there can be meaning in the ways they and others *respond* to what happened.

"What will I do now? How can I help prevent this from happening again? In what ways can I honor the life of the person who died? How can I become a more loving, compassionate, helpful person as a result of this tragedy?" For many survivors of homicide death, these are ultimately the meaning questions that *do* have answers. These are the questions that can eventually lead to peace and a renewed love for life. While you may not be at this place right now in your journey, my hope for you is that you find your way there eventually.

The question of forgiveness often arises when mourners work on this need, as well. Do you have to forgive those who caused or contributed to the death of your loved one to be able to move forward in your grief journey? What if the rules of your religion or spiritual beliefs require forgiveness? I don't believe that forgiveness is necessary for healing. For some survivors, forgiveness is an important milestone in their journeys through grief. The choice to forgive often does lessen survivors' suffering and may bring peace. They feel relieved of a heavy burden. For others, heartfelt forgiveness is not to be. If this applies to you, does this mean you're "stuck" in your grief journey or that you'll never truly heal? I don't believe so. It simply means you have come to a decision about the morality of the death, and that decision itself can bring its own sense of peace. Whichever path you choose, it becomes part of your ongoing journey.

Of course, exploring spiritual and religious beliefs is also part of this need of mourning. You will probably naturally question your philosophy of life as well as religious and spiritual values as you work on this need. Remember that having faith or spirituality does not negate your need to mourn. As the Bible reminds us, "Blessed are those who mourn, for they shall be comforted."

You can intentionally, outwardly work on this need of mourning in any number of ways. Because grief is largely a spiritual quest, I encourage you to spend at least fifteen minutes a day on a practice that engages you spiritually and feeds your soul. For example, you can pray, meditate, do yoga, spend time in nature, attend religious or spiritual services, read spiritual texts, or talk to a friend or spiritual mentor about beliefs and values.

Make the effort to embrace your spirituality and it will embrace you back by helping you move toward hope, peace, and healing.

MOURNING NEED 6: RECEIVE AND ACCEPT HELP FROM OTHERS

As mourners, we need the love and understanding of others if we are to heal. Because homicide grief is so complicated and difficult, this is especially true for you.

We've said that mourning is grief expressed or grief in action. It's also the shared social response to loss. When two or more people grieving the same loss get together to talk about it, comfort one another, share memories, and offer ongoing support, that is a crucial facet of this need of mourning.

I encourage you to reach out to friends and family members

whenever you need a listening ear, could use help with a decision or task, or just want some company. If some of your people seem to have abandoned you, try reaching out anyway. Many are probably at a loss for what to say or do, but if you reach out, some will reach back. Be proactive and appropriately assertive in asking for the help you need and deserve.

Grief support groups, especially those for homicide survivors, can be a lifesaving avenue of support. You might find one that meets face-to-face in your community, or you can join an online group. As you experience the physical separation from the person you love, you are connected to every other person who has experienced a similar loss. As The Compassionate Friends (an international organization of bereaved parents) says, "We need not walk alone."

Your local victims' advocacy organizations and grief counselors can also be excellent sources of support. Remember that your loss is traumatic, and so you have special grief needs. By all means, take advantage of any services in your community that will help you get the help you need.

Grief is a long process, not an event. You will need the continued support of friends, family, and others for months and years to come.

CARING FOR YOURSELF
WHILE YOU MOURN

*"With every act of self-care, your authentic self gets stronger,
and the critical, fearful mind gets weaker. Every act of
self-care is a powerful declaration: I am on my side.
Each day I am more and more on my own side."*
— Susan Weiss Berry

Homicide grief and mourning are exceptionally painful
and challenging. Embracing and expressing your naturally
complicated grief takes courage, fortitude, and generous
doses of self-compassion. Remember that emotional
intensive care we talked about earlier? I want you to
administer painstaking self-care like that—gently, kindly, and
unfailingly.

Actually, it's not just emotional intensive self-care you need.
It's also physical, cognitive, social, and spiritual self-care,
because all of these aspects of yourself have been injured and
need and deserve TLC of their own. So far in this book we've
been talking mostly about emotional self-care, but here I
want to briefly discuss the other aspects of self-care.

CARING FOR YOURSELF PHYSICALLY

Earlier we noted that your body may well be feeling and expressing your grief. Physical symptoms of traumatic grief can be very pronounced and debilitating. If you're not sleeping or feeling well physically, you won't have the energy and stamina you need to engage with your grief and actively mourn.

So I urge you to make good physical self-care a top priority. You don't need to become a nutrition guru or gung-ho athlete. You simply need to take measures to ensure you're getting adequate high-quality sleep most nights, eating nutritious food and drinking enough water, and moving your body most days, such as simply walking and stretching.

CARING FOR YOURSELF COGNITIVELY

In grief, cognitive self-care means giving your brain plenty of breaks and soothing activities. Whatever overstresses you cognitively, do as little of that as possible right now. Your brain is taxed enough by the work of traumatic grief. Offload any overly demanding work or tasks that you can. If there are cognitive challenges that you find soothing, on the other hand—such as puzzles or trivia games—by all means, use them to step away from your grief and relax.

CARING FOR YOURSELF SOCIALLY

In addition to reaching out for and accepting the support of others in your grief (Mourning Need 6), social self-care means spending time on activities that help you feel connected with others without creating any undue stress. Think about ways you can spend time with the friends and family members who are supportive of you as well as those whose company you simply enjoy. Then think about how you can remove any stresses normally associated with such gatherings. Keep things simple. For example, if getting together with your family usually means preparing a big meal, get take-out instead.

CARING FOR YOURSELF SPIRITUALLY

The greater your grief, the greater your need for spiritual self-care. Grief always sets in motion a spiritual quest for meaning and purpose, but in the case of homicide grief, this is especially true. Anything that feeds your spirit counts as spiritual self-care. You might try inspirational readings or affirmations, listening to or playing music, walking in the woods or strolling on a beach, playing with children, or getting up early to watch the sun rise.

Tending to your spirit will not only help you feel more even-keeled and happier on a day-to day basis, it will help you create new life-affirming habits as well as discover renewed purpose in your life. Just a little regular spiritual self-care can create powerful ripples of hope and meaning in your life. Give it a try.

WORKING TOWARD RECONCILIATION

"She was no longer wrestling with the grief but could sit down with it as a lasting companion and make it a sharer in her thoughts."
— George Eliot

Healing in grief means "to make whole again." It doesn't mean curing, fixing, or resolving. I'm sure you know by now that your grief can't be cured. You are forever changed by this death. Your life will never be the same. Your grief will never truly end. But you can be whole again, even though it will be a different and patchwork whole.

In my role as grief educator and counselor, I often help mourners understand that what they are working toward when they actively engage with the six needs of mourning is reconciliation of their grief. They are finding ways to integrate their grief and loss into their ongoing life and live the rest of their days with connection, meaning, and purpose. The word "reconcile" comes from the Middle English for "to make good again." This is the essence of reconciliation in grief, actually—to make your life good again.

You'll know that you're moving toward reconciling your grief when it starts to feel like an integral part of your life story. You will feel that your relationship with the person who died has changed from one of presence to one of memory (and perhaps one of hoped-for eventual reunion). You will continue to feel both parts of your two-part grief sometimes, but the part focusing on the manner of the death will no longer be so intense or prominent.

Slowly and over time, as you begin to reconcile your grief, you will begin to notice:

- A return to stable eating and sleeping patterns.

- A sense of release from or acceptance of the event of the death.

- The capacity to enjoy experiences in life that are normally enjoyable.

- The capacity to live a full life without feelings of guilt or shame.

- The drive to organize and plan your life toward the future.

- The serenity to become comfortable with the way things are rather than attempting to make things as they were.

Grief after Homicide

- The versatility to welcome more change in life.

- The awareness that nobody "gets over" grief; instead, you have a new reality, meaning, and purpose in your life.

In grief, reconciliation emerges much in the way grass grows. Usually we don't check our lawns daily to see if the grass is growing, but it does grow and soon we come to realize it's time to mow the grass again. Likewise, we don't look at ourselves each day as mourners to see how we are healing. Yet we do come to realize, over the course of months and years, that we have come a long way.

As you work your way through the wilderness of your homicide grief toward reconciliation, you will hopefully begin to find ongoing purpose in some aspect of your loved one's life or death. For example, you may decide to finish something that your loved one left unfinished or support a cause that was meaningful to them. Or maybe you'd like to explore creating a scholarship, funding or volunteering for a charity, or hosting an annual gathering of others who knew and loved this special person. Perhaps you'll simply live forward in ways that you know your loved one would be proud of.

A FINAL WORD

"Your body is away from me, but there is a window open from my heart to yours."

— Rumi

There are no words that can take away your pain or do your work of mourning for you. But I hope the thoughts in this little book have helped you understand your unique two-part grief a bit better and begin to think about ways to embrace and express it in manageable doses.

Never forget that your grief is your love for the person who died, only in a different form. It's normal and natural. Even more, like love, it's sacred And the more you befriend it, the more you will see that it's nothing to be afraid of.

The six needs of mourning are how you express your grief. They, too, are your friends. The more you actively work with them, the more momentum they will give your grief toward hope and healing.

The many homicide grievers I have companioned over the years have one last message for you: You deserve to live the rest of your precious days with as much authenticity, joy, meaning, and purpose as possible. Befriending and mourning your grief well is what will allow you to live well and love well again.

Right now, I invite you to close your eyes and call to mind the best smile of the person who died. This is what they want for you. Godspeed.

THE HOMICIDE GRIEVER'S BILL OF RIGHTS

by Alan D. Wolfelt, Ph.D.

You have been injured by great loss. As a homicide griever, you have certain rights that bear repeating and upholding.

1. YOU HAVE THE RIGHT TO EMOTIONAL AND SPIRITUAL INTENSIVE CARE.

Homicide creates a two-part grief experience like no other. You have been deeply wounded by a traumatic loss, and you need and deserve emotional and spiritual intensive care.

2. YOU HAVE THE RIGHT TO FEEL SAFE.

The manner of this death may have made you feel anxious and unsafe. You may be experiencing some degree of post-traumatic stress. You have the right to get extra help and to do whatever you need to do to feel safe again.

3. YOU HAVE THE RIGHT TO EXPERIENCE YOUR OWN UNIQUE GRIEF.

No one else will grieve in exactly the same way you do. So, when you turn to others for help, don't allow them to tell you what you should or should not be feeling.

4. YOU HAVE THE RIGHT TO TALK ABOUT YOUR GRIEF.

You have the right to talk about both the cause of the death and the forever loss of the person who died. Talking about your grief will help you heal. Seek out others who will allow you to talk as much as you want, as often as you want, about both parts of your grief. If at times you don't feel like talking, you also have the right to be silent.

5. YOU HAVE THE RIGHT TO FEEL WHATEVER YOU FEEL.

Shock, numbness, confusion, disorientation, fear, guilt, and sadness are just a few of the emotions you might feel as part of your grief journey. Others may try to tell you that certain feelings—anger, for example—are wrong. Don't take these judgmental responses to heart. Instead, find listeners who will accept your feelings without judgment.

6. YOU HAVE THE RIGHT TO BE TOLERANT OF YOUR PHYSICAL AND EMOTIONAL LIMITS.

Your feelings of trauma and loss will probably leave you feeling fatigued. Respect what your body and mind are telling you. Get daily rest. Eat balanced meals. And don't allow others to push you into doing things you don't feel ready to do.

7. YOU HAVE THE RIGHT TO EMBRACE YOUR SPIRITUALITY.

Express your spirituality in ways that feel right to you. Allow yourself to be around people who understand and support your religious or spiritual beliefs. If you feel angry at God, find someone to talk with who won't be critical of your feelings of hurt and abandonment.

8. YOU HAVE THE RIGHT TO SEARCH FOR MEANING.

You may find yourself asking, "Why did they die? Why in this way? Why do bad things happen to good people?" Some of your questions may have answers, but some may not. And watch out for the clichéd responses some people may give you. Comments like, "It was God's will" or "Think of what you have to be thankful for" are not helpful and you do not have to accept them.

9. YOU HAVE THE RIGHT TO TREASURE YOUR MEMORIES.

It's true that the person who died will live on in you through memory. Memories are one of the best legacies that exist after the death of someone loved. Instead of avoiding your memories, intentionally befriend them, and find others with whom you can share them.

10. YOU HAVE THE RIGHT TO MOVE TOWARD YOUR GRIEF AND HEAL.

Reconciling your homicide grief will not happen quickly. Remember, there are no rewards for speed. Be patient and tolerant with yourself and avoid people who are impatient and intolerant with you. Neither you nor those around you must forget that the homicide death of someone loved changes your life forever.

Understanding Your Grief After a Drug-Overdose Death

In this compassionate guide, Dr. Alan Wolfelt shares the most important lessons he has learned from loved ones who've picked up the pieces in the aftermath of a drug overdose.

ISBN: 978-1-61722-285-6 • softcover • **$9.95**

Too Much Loss: Coping with Grief Overload

Grief overload is what you feel when you experience too many significant losses all at once, in a relatively short period of time, or cumulatively. Our minds and hearts have enough trouble coping with a single loss, so when the losses pile up, the grief often seems especially chaotic and defeating.

ISBN: 978-1-61722-287-0 • softcover • **$9.95**

The Grief of Infertility

When you want to have a baby but are struggling with fertility challenges, it's normal to experience a range and mixture of ever-changing feelings. These feelings are a natural and necessary form of grief.

ISBN: 978-1-61722-291-7 • softcover • **$9.95**

Expected Loss: Coping with Anticipatory Grief

We don't only experience grief after a loss—we often experience it before. If someone we love is seriously ill, or if we're concerned about upcoming hardships of any kind, we naturally begin to grieve right now. This process of anticipatory grief is normal, but it can also be confusing and painful.

ISBN: 978-1-61722-295-5 • softcover • **$9.95**

Nature Heals: Reconciling Your Grief Through Engaging with the Natural World

When we're grieving, we need relief from our pain. Today we often turn to technology for distraction when what we really need is the opposite: generous doses of nature. Studies show that time spent outdoors lowers blood pressure, eases depression and anxiety, bolsters the immune system, lessens stress, and even makes us more compassionate. This guide to the tonic of nature explores why engaging with the natural world is so effective at helping reconcile grief.

978-1-61722-301-3 • softcover • $9.95

Sympathy and Condolences: What to Say and Write to Convey Your Support After a Loss

When someone you care about has suffered the death of a loved one or another significant loss, you want to let them know you care. But it can be hard to know what to say to them or to write in a sympathy note. This handy book offers tips for how to talk or write to a grieving person to convey your genuine concern and support.

978-1-61722-305-1 • $9.95 • softcover

All Dr. Wolfelt's publications can be ordered by mail from:
Companion Press, 3735 Broken Bow Road, Fort Collins, CO 80526
(970) 226-6050 • www.centerforloss.com

ABOUT THE AUTHOR

Alan D. Wolfelt, Ph.D., is a respected author and educator on the topics of companioning others and healing in grief. He serves as Director of the Center for Loss and Life Transition and is on the faculty at the University of Colorado Medical

 School's Department of Family Medicine. Dr. Wolfelt has written many bestselling books on healing in grief, including *Understanding Your Grief, Healing Your Grieving Heart*, and *The Mourner's Book of Hope*. Visit www.centerforloss.com to learn more about grief and loss and to order Dr. Wolfelt's books.